Looking at Minibeasts

Slugs and Snails

Sally Morgan

Thameside Press

Contents

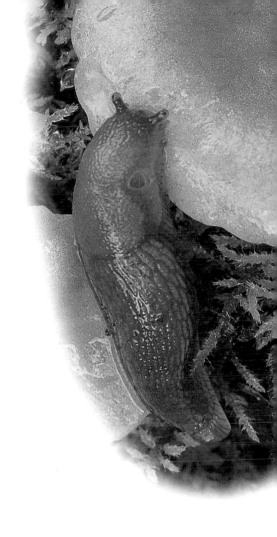

Words in **bold** are
explained on page 31.

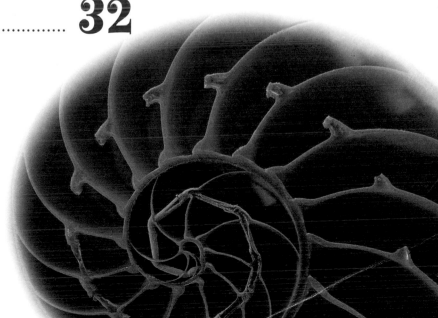

Slugs and snails

Slugs and snails are part of a group of animals called **mollusks**. Most mollusks have a **shell**. A snail carries its shell on its back. A slug has a tiny shell hidden inside its body. Both animals glide along slowly on a large **foot**. This is a flat muscle on the underside of the slug or snail.

A snail has a hard shell and a soft body.

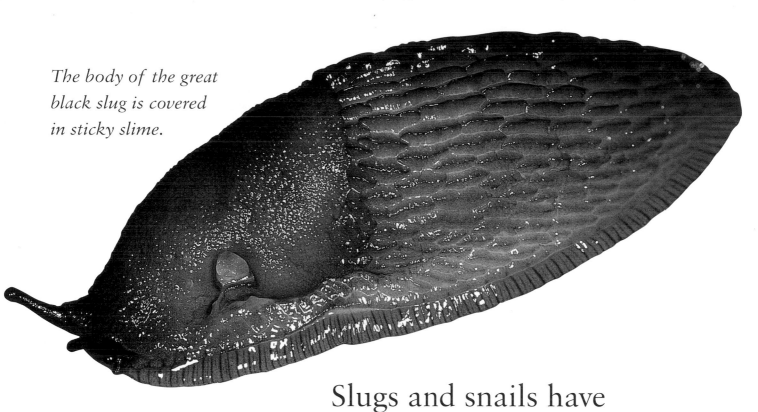

The body of the great black slug is covered in sticky slime.

Slugs and snails have two long **tentacles** and two short tentacles on their heads. The long tentacles are for seeing. The short tentacles are for smelling and tasting.

The giant snail lives in rain forests. It glides across the forest floor.

The snail family

Some mollusks live in gardens and parks, but many more live in ponds, rivers, and oceans. The snail's largest relatives are squid, cuttlefish, and octopuses. These mollusks live in the sea. They have long tentacles which may be covered in **suckers**. Their shells are hidden inside their bodies.

This brightly-colored sea slug lives in water.

*The cuttlefish
has 10 tentacles on
the front of its head.*

The members of the
snail family vary in
size. Glass snails are
less than ¼ inch (6 mm)
long. The giant squid is one
of the largest mollusks. It
grows up to 70 feet (20m) long.

*Mussels are mollusks
which live on the
seashore. They attach
themselves to the rocks.*

Living in a shell

A snail's shell is made of a hard material like chalk. The shell protects the snail's soft body. When the snail is frightened or under attack from another animal, it pulls its body into the shell. As the snail grows, it has to make more shell.

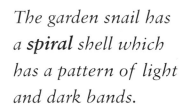

*The garden snail has a **spiral** shell which has a pattern of light and dark bands.*

A snail stretches out its body while it is moving or feeding (left).

A snail adds new material to the edge of its shell to make it larger. If the shell is a **spiral**, the spiral gets larger and larger.

If you touch a snail, it pulls its body back into its shell (above).

A hermit crab does not have a shell of its own. Instead, it lives in the shell of a dead sea snail.

Shell shapes

Snail shells are many shapes and sizes. Some shells are cone-shaped. Other shells have a spiral pattern. Mussels, scallops, oysters, and clams are mollusks that live in the sea. They are **bivalves**. This means they have two shells joined together. Bivalves can open and close their shells, just like opening and closing a door.

The conch is a type of snail. It has one of the largest shells.

This scallop is a bivalve, because it has two shells.

Shells can be many colors. Most land snails have brown shells. Sea snails often have brightly-colored shells. Some shells have spots and stripes.

When a snail shell is cut in half, you can see a spiral which winds round and round.

Land and water

Slugs and snails like damp, shady places such as woods. Here they can hide under logs and leaves. Only a few types of slugs and snails live in hot, dry parts of the world.

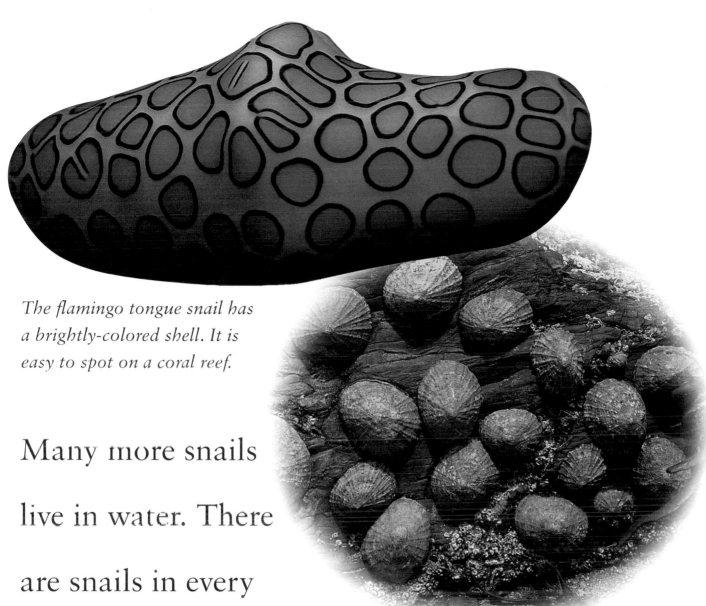

The flamingo tongue snail has a brightly-colored shell. It is easy to spot on a coral reef.

Limpets attach themselves to rocks on a beach. They can live underwater and out of the water.

Many more snails live in water. There are snails in every pond. Colorful tropical snails live on **coral reefs**. You can find snails on the beach too—in **tide pools** and under the sand.

Moving over land

Slugs and snails move very slowly, using a flat muscle called a foot. The foot is a large part of the body of a slug or snail. Its underside is covered in a slimy **mucus**. This helps the animal to glide over the ground.

The foot of this snail is twice as long as its shell.

The underside of a snail's foot is flat and covered in mucus.

Everywhere they go, snails and slugs leave behind a shining trail of dried mucus.

Moving in water

Pond snails use a foot to move too. They glide across the surface of the water and climb over plants. Larger mollusks move in different ways. Scallops are **bivalves** which jump across the seabed if another animal tries to attack them.

This scallop is jumping across the sea floor.

The squid and the octopus move by shooting out a powerful jet of water. The jet pushes the animal backward through the water.

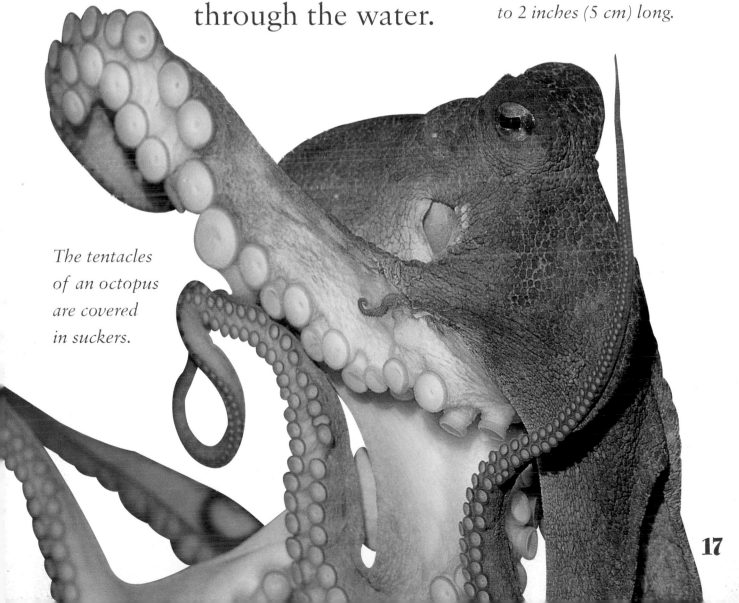

The great pond snail (above) can grow up to 2 inches (5 cm) long.

The tentacles of an octopus are covered in suckers.

Hundreds of teeth

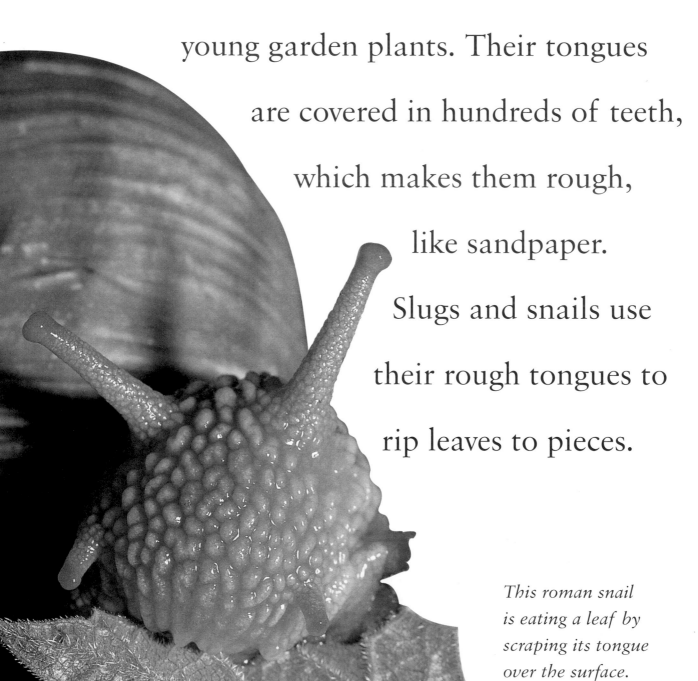

Snails and slugs are **pests** because they like to eat young garden plants. Their tongues are covered in hundreds of teeth, which makes them rough, like sandpaper. Slugs and snails use their rough tongues to rip leaves to pieces.

This roman snail is eating a leaf by scraping its tongue over the surface.

Animals that eat plants are called **herbivores**. Most slugs and snails are herbivores, but a few are **predators**. Predators feed on other animals.

Slugs (right) eat fruits, leaves, and the shoots of plants.

Dogwinkles are predators. They use their tongues to drill through the shells of other snails.

Under attack

Many animals like to eat slugs and snails.
The thrush catches a snail in its beak. Then it
crushes the snail's shell by hitting it hard against
a stone. When the shell is
in pieces, the thrush
can eat the soft
body inside.
The thrush uses
the same stone
again and again. Around the stone are the
broken shells of all the snails it has eaten.

Sometimes snails are attacked by ants. The ants kill the snail by biting its soft body.

Sea slugs are very brightly colored. The colors are a warning to other animals to stay away. Parts of a sea slug's body are covered with **sting cells**. The slug protects itself from predators by firing poison-tipped threads from its sting cells.

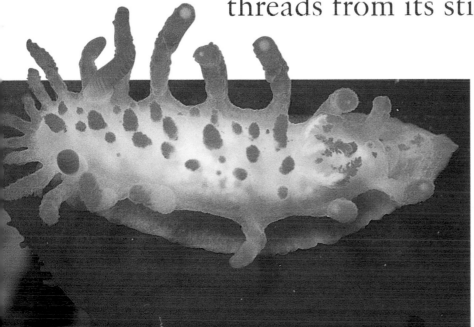

The sea slug is poisonous. Its bright colors scare off attackers.

21

Night animals

During the day, snails and slugs hide under logs, pots, and stones. They come out at night, when it is cooler. They like the warm, damp evenings of the spring and fall. If you go outside with a flashlight on a damp evening, you may see hundreds of snails looking for food.

These snails are hiding in an old plant pot during the day.

The opening of this snail's shell is sealed up with mucus.

Snails often cluster on fence posts in hot weather. They stay there until wet weather returns.

Snails may dry up in very hot weather. They seal up the opening of their shells with a thick layer of mucus. This stops water from leaving their bodies.

Finding their way

Slugs and snails use their tentacles to find their way around. A snail has two pairs of tentacles at the front of its head. The shorter pair is for tasting and smelling. Each of the long tentacles has a simple eye at the end.

Snails cannot see as well as we can, but they can **detect** light. This means that a snail can move towards or away from light.

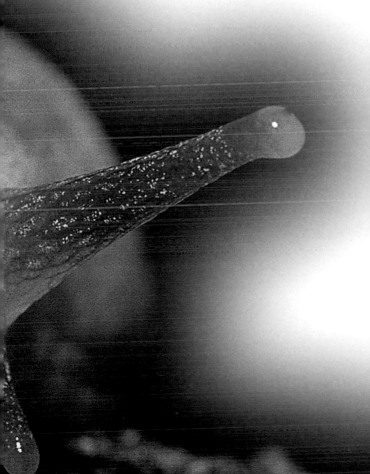

Pond snails use their tentacles to find food in the water.

From egg to adult

Land snails lay small, white eggs in holes in the ground. They may lay as many as 40 eggs in each hole. After four weeks, tiny baby snails hatch out. They start feeding at once, and grow very quickly.

1. Snails lay tiny white eggs in the soil.

2. Miniature snails hatch from the eggs. As they grow, their shells grow too.

Pond snails lay their eggs on pond weeds. The eggs are covered in a jelly. This stops other animals from eating the eggs.

This blob of jelly contains many pond snail eggs.

3. A snail may take two years to reach adult size. Some snails live as long as 10 years.

3

Watching minibeasts

Slugs and snails are found in damp, shady places—such as under pots, logs, and stones. Look for them on a warm, damp evening. You can catch slugs and snails by making a trap out of a grapefruit skin.

The animals creep under the skin during the day. Trapped slugs and snails can be kept in a damp, shady fish tank. Ask an adult to help you put soil and leaves into the

To make a slug trap, rest one edge of a grapefruit skin on a stone.

tank. Then add a few moss-covered twigs and stones. Make sure the tank has a lid to stop the animals from escaping. The snails will eat leafy vegetables such as lettuce.

If you keep snails in a fish tank, put them back where you found them after a few weeks.

Snails and slugs are safe to handle. Look at them with a magnifying glass, or ask an adult to place a slug or snail on a sheet of Perspex. You can watch the animal move from beneath the sheet.

You can see how snails behave in the wild by painting numbers on their shells. Then put them back in the garden. You can find out where the snails hide, how far they move, and what they like to eat.

Always ask an adult to make sure the paint is non-toxic and does not touch the snail's body.

Minibeast sizes

Slugs and snails are many sizes. The pictures in this book do not show them at their actual size. Below you can see how big they are in real life.

Garden snail shell
1½ inches (4 cm) wide

Sea slug
1½ inches (4 cm) long

Dogwinkle shell
¾ inch (2 cm) wide

Great black slug
up to 6 inches (150 mm) long

Glossary

bivalve A mollusk that has two shells.

coral reef A hard wall made by sea animals called coral.

detect To find out or discover.

foot The flat part of a slug or snail, used for moving around.

herbivore An animal that eats only plants.

mollusk An animal with a soft body and a shell.

mucus A thick, sticky slime.

pest An animal that damages crops.

predator An animal that hunts and eats other animals.

shell A hard outer covering.

spiral A curve that winds round and round on itself.

sting cells Parts of an animal that make poisonous stings.

suckers Round shapes on an animal's body that grip things.

tentacles The feelers of a snail, or the arms of an octopus or squid.

tide pool A pool of seawater trapped between rocks on a beach.

Index

Distributed in the United States by
Smart Apple Media
1980 Lookout Drive
North Mankato, MN 56003

Text copyright © Sally Morgan 2000
Illustrations by Woody

Editor: Russell McLean
Designers: John Jamieson, Ian Butterworth
Picture researcher: Sally Morgan
Educational consultant: Emma Harvey

ISBN: 1-929298-81-1

Printed in the USA

9 8 7 6 5 4 3 2

Library of Congress Cataloging-in-Publication Data

Morgan, Sally.
    Slugs and snails / by Sally Morgan.
        p. cm. -- (Looking at minibeasts)
    Summary: Describes slugs and snails in their natural habitats, with information on how to observe these creatures without harming them or their environment.
        ISBN 1-929298-81-1
    1. Slugs (Mollusks)--Juvenile literature. 2. Snails--Juvenile literature. [1. Slugs (Mollusks). 2. Snails.] I. Title.

QL430.4 .M77 2000
594'.38--dc21   00-024942

Picture acknowledgements: Jeff Collett/Ecoscene: 3b, 7t, 11b. Anthony Cooper/Ecoscene: 22. W. Lawler/Ecoscene: 10b. John Liddiard/Ecoscene: 6b, 16. OSF: 20. Papilio: front cover b, 2, 3t, 9b, 14, 17b, 19t, 23t, 25t, 25c. Robert Pickett/Papilio: front & back cover tcr & tr, 5t, 13t, 15r, 17t, 23b, 27t, 30. Ken Preston-Mafham/Premaphotos: front cover tcl & c, back cover tcl, 1, 4b, 5b, 8b, 9t, 9c, 11t, 12, 13c, 18, 21t, 24-25, 26bl, 26br, 27b, 30cl, 30cr. Rod Preston-Mafham/Premaphotos: front & back cover tl, 19b, 21b, 30bl, 30c. Barrie Watts: 7c, 15l.